Fantasy & Horror Pinup Coloring Book

by Richard McConochie

www.ingramcontent.com/pod-product-compliance
Lightning Source LLC
Chambersburg PA
CBHW081642220526
45468CB00009B/2528
* 9 7 8 1 7 2 4 5 1 1 8 3 6 *